Practicing for STAAR Success

Grade 3 Reading

Author
Jennifer Prior

Introduction Author

Delia E. Racines, Ph.D.
Faculty, University of Southern California
USC Language Academy

Publishing Credits

Corinne Burton, M.A.Ed., *President*; Conni Medina, M.A.Ed., *Managing Editor*; Emily R. Smith, M.A.Ed., *Content Director*; Aubrie Nielsen, M.S.Ed., *Content Director*; Debra J. Housel, M.S.Ed., *Editor*; Jennifer Wilson, *Editor*; Kat Bernardo, M.Ed., *Editor*; Reha Jain, M.Ed., *Editor*; Courtney Patterson, *Multimedia Designer*; Don Tran, *Graphic Designer*; Tara Hurley, *Editorial Assistant*

Image Credits

All images Shutterstock unless noted otherwise.

Standards

© Copyright 2007–2015. Texas Education Association (TEA). All rights reserved.

Shell Education

a division of Teacher Created Materials
5301 Oceanus Drive
Huntington Beach, CA 92649-1030
ISBN 978-1-4258-1705-3
http://www.tcmpub.com/shell-education

Table of Contents

Introduction

Today's Next Generation Tests 4

How to Use This Resource 7

Making It Meaningful 9

Informational Practice Exercises

Bats on the Brink 11

The Scoop on Sugar 16

A Woman Up a Tree 22

The Coral Reef Crisis 27

Undersea Volcanoes 32

She Gives Them Food for Thought 37

For Sale: Rare and Stolen Pets 41

Threads of Kindness 46

Literature Practice Exercises

The Long Trail 50

Paul Bunyan 54

Go Fly a Kite! 58

A Bedouin Tale 63

The Lion and the Wild Boar 68

Racing a Tornado 72

The Treasure Hunt 77

It's a Dog's Life 82

Poetry Practice Exercises

Windy Nights 87

A Pleasant Day 91

The Plumpuppets 95

Mr. Macklin's Jack O'Lantern 99

Appendices

Appendix A: Answer Sheet 103

Appendix B: Correlation to Assessed Standards 104

Appendix C: Testing Tips 108

Appendix D: References Cited 110

Appendix E: Answer Key 111

Today's Next Generation Tests

> "To be college and career ready, students must now read across a broad range of high-quality texts from diverse cultures and times in history."
>
> —Delia E. Racines, Ph.D.

Education is currently undergoing a dramatic shift when it comes to the ways we measure and assess for learning. Educational standards across the nation are designed to provide clear and meaningful goals for our students. These standards serve as a frame of reference for educators, parents, and students and are most critical when decisions must be made about curriculum, textbooks, assessments, and other aspects of instructional programs (Conley 2014). Part of the disconnect with standards in the recent past has been the vast differences in expectations. This lack of consistency became a major concern for the quality of education students were receiving across the country (Conley 2014; Wiley and Wright 2004).

Standards in education in the United States are not a new concept. However, the role of educational standards has recently shifted to not only ensure that all students have access to equitable education no matter where they live, but also to ensure a more consistent national expectation for what all students should know to be successful in a rapidly changing economy and society (Kornhaber, Griffith, and Tyler 2014).

Scales, scores, and assessments are absolutely necessary to ascertain the current status of students. This kind of data is vital for teachers to understand what is missing and what the next steps should be. The real question about assessment isn't whether we should assess but rather what kinds of assessments should be used. Along with the current shift to more consistent and rigorous standards, states now measure student progress with assessments that require higher-order thinking skills necessary for preparation for college and/or careers.

So, what is this new yardstick that is being used? How is it better than yardsticks of the past? And how do we best prepare students to be measured with this yardstick in a way that tells the whole story?

The following description serves to explain the format of the STAAR program, which was developed and adopted by the Texas School Board of Education, and replaced the previously administered Texas Assessment of Knowledge and Skills (TAKS).

Today's Next Generation Tests *(cont.)*

The State of Texas Assessment of Academic Readiness (STAAR) Program

The STAAR program was implemented in 2012 by the Texas Education Agency (TEA) to assess the Texas Essential Knowledge and Skills (TEKS). These assessments focus on readiness for college and/or careers with test questions that focus on rigor and critical analysis.

At the elementary and middle school levels, the English Language Arts and Reading TEKS are assessed with two tests: STAAR Reading and STAAR Writing. STAAR Reading is given to students each year in grades 3–8, while STAAR Writing is administered in grades 4 and 7 only. STAAR Spanish Reading is offered in grades 3–5, and STAAR Spanish Writing is administered in grade 4. Additional tests within the STAAR program include STAAR L, a language-modified assessment for eligible English language learners, and STAAR A, an online version with embedded accommodations for students with disabilities (Texas Education Agency 2014).

The general STAAR and STAAR Spanish assessments are available on paper only. The question format is multiple-choice, and students record their answers on an answer sheet. Students must complete the assessment within four hours, unless students meet the criteria for accommodations of extra time (Texas Education Agency 2014).

Students' scores on STAAR are reported as one of three categories:

- Level III: Advanced Academic Performance
- Level II: Satisfactory Academic Performance
- Level I: Unsatisfactory Academic Performance

Level II is considered the passing standard on STAAR, so students scoring at Level II or Level III have passed, while students scoring at Level 1 have not passed (Texas Education Agency 2014).

Today's Next Generation Tests (cont.)

The State of Texas Assessment of Academic Readiness (STAAR) Program (cont.)

Reporting Categories in STAAR Reading

The Texas Education Agency has identified certain TEKS that are eligible for assessment on STAAR Reading and has defined three reporting categories for those standards: *Understanding Across Genres*, *Understanding and Analysis of Literary Texts*, and *Understanding and Analysis of Informational Texts*. A brief description of the reporting categories is provided below. For a complete list of the TEKS evaluated in each reporting category, visit the TEA website at www.tea.texas.gov.

Reporting Category 1: Understanding Across Genres

Reporting Category 1 assesses students' ability to comprehend various texts from different genres, including fiction, literary nonfiction, poetry, drama (grade 4 and up), expository, persuasive (grade 5 and up), procedural, and media literacy. The questions in this category focus on the TEKS that cover vocabulary development and comprehension skills.

Reporting Category 2: Understanding and Analysis of Literary Texts

The questions in Reporting Category 2 assess how well students are able to understand and analyze literary texts. Students must be able to apply comprehension skills to draw conclusions and make inferences about literary themes, plot, characters, text structures, sensory language, point of view, and author's purpose. Students are also expected to accurately summarize texts and provide evidence from a text to support their conclusions and inferences.

Reporting Category 3: Understanding and Analysis of Informational Texts

Reporting Category 3 poses questions that assess students' ability to comprehend and analyze informational texts. As with the Reporting Category 2 questions, students must be able to summarize and cite text evidence to support their responses to texts. The TEKS that focus on informational texts ask students to identify a text's main idea and supporting details, differentiate fact from opinion, identify text structures and features, and use information in graphic features.

Readiness Standards versus Supporting Standards

In the process of developing the STAAR Program, the TEA made a distinction between "Readiness" and "Supporting" standards for the TEKS that are eligible for assessment. Those standards that have been designated as "Readiness" are considered the most crucial for success with the curriculum and have a heavier focus in STAAR tests. While the "Supporting" standards are deemed important for instruction, they may or may not be tested each year.

How to Use This Resource

The practice exercises in this resource have been designed to offer students the opportunity to prepare for STAAR Reading by providing questions aligned to the eligible TEKS and in a style and format that mirrors STAAR tests.

In order to succeed on STAAR, students must be able to correctly record answers on a separate answer sheet. While the practice exercises in this book can certainly be used without the answer sheet, including it as part of test preparation gives students practice with properly filling in bubbles and finding the correct location to record an answer for each test item.

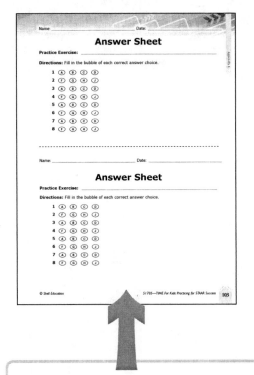

Make copies of the answer sheet and cut them in half on the dotted line. Have students use a half-sheet to record their answers for each practice exercise.

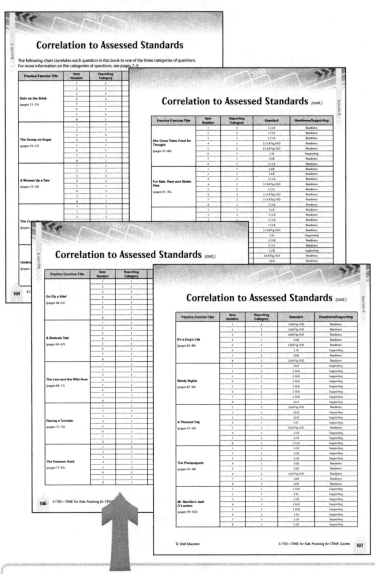

The Correlation to Assessed Standards on pages 99–102 provides information on the reporting category, standard, and type of standard (Readiness or Supporting) for each test item.

Making It Meaningful

The section has been included to make this book's test practice more meaningful. The purpose of this section is to provide sample guiding questions framed around a specific practice exercise. This will serve as a meaningful and real-life application of the test practice. Each of the guiding questions serves as a thinking prompt to ensure that all categories of the reading standards have been considered. The guiding questions may be used with students as a teacher-led think aloud or to individually assess how students are approaching and understanding complex texts. The framework used in this model serves as a template for how to approach other fiction and nonfiction texts. The template supports educators in preparing students for today's tests and helps make meaning of the reading standards to ultimately ensure that the learning becomes more meaningful for all students.

Begin asking students these questions:

What type of text is this?

What is the purpose of this type of text?

Identify what text structures are used in this text and why.

What is the relationship among certain vocabulary words?

How do the words shape the tone?

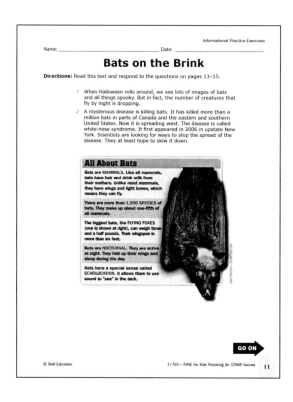

Then, coach students to do the following:

Underline the key details you have noticed so far.

Write a summary sentence with these details as support.

List or create a timeline of important events in the character's story.

Finally, check for understanding by asking students to do the following:

Make connections across other content areas.

Explain how varied ideas relate to one another.

Making It Meaningful (cont.)

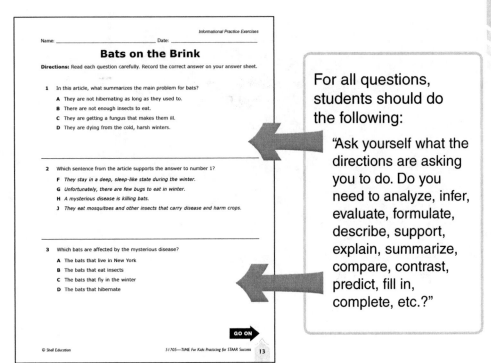

Name: _____ Date: _____

Bats on the Brink

Directions: Read each question carefully. Record the correct answer on your answer sheet.

1   In this article, what summarizes the main problem for bats?

   A They are not hibernating as long as they used to.

   B There are not enough insects to eat.

   C They are getting a fungus that makes them ill.

   D They are dying from the cold, harsh winters.

2   Which sentence from the article supports the answer to number 1?

   F *They stay in a deep, sleep-like state during the winter.*

   G *Unfortunately, there are few bugs to eat in winter.*

   H *A mysterious disease is killing bats.*

   J *They eat mosquitoes and other insects that carry disease and harm crops.*

3   Which bats are affected by the mysterious disease?

   A The bats that live in New York

   B The bats that eat insects

   C The bats that fly in the winter

   D The bats that hibernate

GO ON

© Shell Education   51705—TIME For Kids: Practicing for STAAR Success   **13**

For all questions, students should do the following:

"Ask yourself what the directions are asking you to do. Do you need to analyze, infer, evaluate, formulate, describe, support, explain, summarize, compare, contrast, predict, fill in, complete, etc.?"

When answers refer to specific sentences in the text, guide students in the following way:

"These answers reference specific sentences in the text. Go back and find these sentences. Then, reread the text around the sentences to find out which one is the answer to the question."

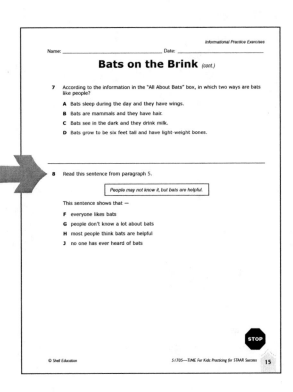

Name: _____ Date: _____

Bats on the Brink (cont.)

7   According to the information in the "All About Bats" box, in which two ways are bats like people?

   A Bats sleep during the day and they have wings.

   B Bats are mammals and they have hair.

   C Bats see in the dark and they drink milk.

   D Bats grow to be six feet tall and have light-weight bones.

8   Read this sentence from paragraph 5.

> People may not know it, but bats are helpful.

This sentence shows that —

   F everyone likes bats

   G people don't know a lot about bats

   H most people think bats are helpful

   J no one has ever heard of bats

STOP

© Shell Education   51705—TIME For Kids: Practicing for STAAR Success   **15**

Making It Meaningful *(cont.)*

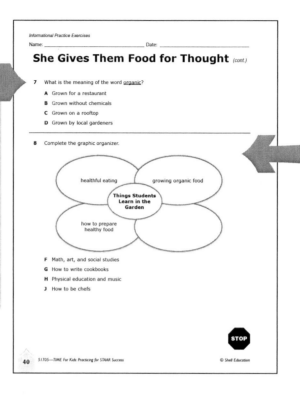

When students are asked vocabulary questions, help them in the following way:

"Find the specific vocabulary word in the text and circle it. Use the other words around it to figure out its meaning using context clues."

If students need to complete graphic organizers, use guiding questions to help them determine how the text can help them respond.

"What does the chart say about bats being like people? Find the text in the chart and use it to answer the question."

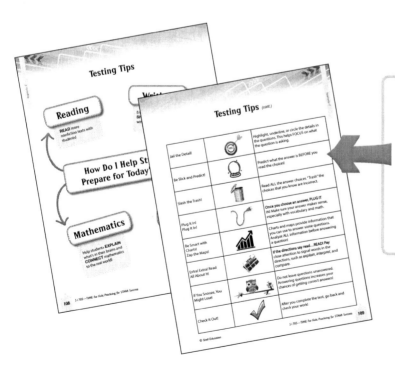

To support students in preparing for today's tests, send home the Testing Tips flyers on pages 108–109. One page is intended to guide parents as they help prepare their children. The second page helps students understand ways they can be more successful while taking tests.

Name: _____ Date: _____

Bats on the Brink

Directions: Read this text and respond to the questions on pages 13–15.

1 When Halloween rolls around, we see lots of images of bats and all things spooky. But in fact, the number of creatures that fly by night is dropping.

2 A mysterious disease is killing bats. It has killed more than a million bats in parts of Canada and the eastern and southern United States. Now it is spreading west. The disease is called white-nose syndrome. It first appeared in 2006 in upstate New York. Scientists are looking for ways to stop the spread of the disease. They at least hope to slow it down.

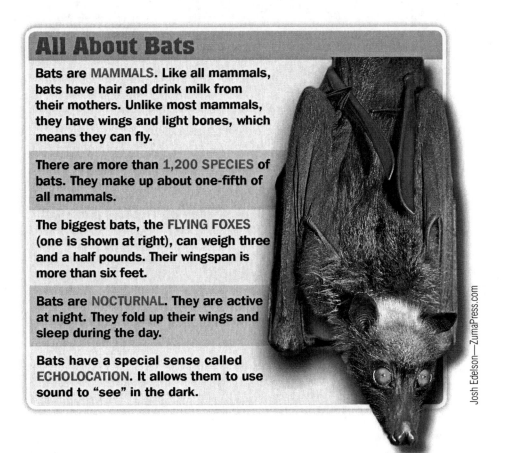

All About Bats

Bats are MAMMALS. Like all mammals, bats have hair and drink milk from their mothers. Unlike most mammals, they have wings and light bones, which means they can fly.

There are more than 1,200 SPECIES of bats. They make up about one-fifth of all mammals.

The biggest bats, the FLYING FOXES (one is shown at right), can weigh three and a half pounds. Their wingspan is more than six feet.

Bats are NOCTURNAL. They are active at night. They fold up their wings and sleep during the day.

Bats have a special sense called ECHOLOCATION. It allows them to use sound to "see" in the dark.

Josh Edelson—ZumaPress.com

GO ON

Name: _____ Date: _____

Bats on the Brink

Saving the Species

3 Some bats hibernate. They stay in a deep, sleep-like state during the winter. Only hibernating bats seem to get white-nose syndrome. Scientists think that the disease is caused by a fungus. The fungus grows on a bat's nose, wings, and ears. It hurts wing <u>tissues</u>. It may make the bats uncomfortable. That causes them to end their hibernation early. When they do, they burn up fat stored in their bodies. Bats need fat to survive the winter. Unfortunately, there are few bugs to eat in winter. With nothing to eat, many of the bats starve.

4 Researchers are testing drugs to fight the fungus. They told TIME For Kids that more money is needed. The money would be used to study the disease and find a cure. "It's important to save bats," says scientist Mollie Matteson. "They are fascinating animals. We can learn a lot from them."

5 People may not know it, but bats are helpful. They eat mosquitoes and other insects that carry disease and harm crops. "Bats are our friends," says bat expert Tom Kunz. "They help people and the environment they live in."

Name: _____ Date: _____

Bats on the Brink

Directions: Read each question carefully. Record the correct answer on your answer sheet.

1   In this article, what summarizes the main problem for bats?

   A They are not hibernating as long as they used to.

   B There are not enough insects to eat.

   C They are getting a fungus that makes them ill.

   D They are dying from the cold, harsh winters.

2   Which sentence from the article supports the answer to number 1?

   F *They stay in a deep, sleep-like state during the winter.*

   G *Unfortunately, there are few bugs to eat in winter.*

   H *A mysterious disease is killing bats.*

   J *They eat mosquitoes and other insects that carry disease and harm crops.*

3   Which bats are affected by the mysterious disease?

   A The bats that live in New York

   B The bats that eat insects

   C The bats that fly in the winter

   D The bats that hibernate

GO ON

Name: _____ Date: _____

Bats on the Brink *(cont.)*

4 The author's point of view is communicated in which sentence?

   F *Scientists are looking for ways to stop the spread of the disease.*

   G *The disease is called white-nose syndrome.*

   H *Some bats hibernate.*

   J *People may not know it, but bats are helpful.*

---

5 Read this dictionary entry.

> **tissue** \tish-oo\ *noun*
> **1.** soft gauzy paper
> **2.** thin writing paper
> **3.** woven fabric
> **4.** skin

Which meaning of <u>tissues</u> is used in paragraph 3?

   A Meaning 1

   B Meaning 2

   C Meaning 3

   D Meaning 4

---

6 The author includes the information inside the "All About Bats" box to —

   F provide more details about bats

   G tell more about the mysterious disease

   H explain why bats are important

   J show different kinds of bats

Name: _____ Date: _____

Bats on the Brink *(cont.)*

7 According to the information in the "All About Bats" box, in which two ways are bats like people?

   A Bats sleep during the day and they have wings.

   B Bats are mammals and they have hair.

   C Bats see in the dark and they drink milk.

   D Bats grow to be six feet tall and have lightweight bones.

---

8 Read this sentence from paragraph 5.

> *People may not know it, but bats are helpful.*

This sentence shows that —

   F everyone likes bats

   G people don't know a lot about bats

   H most people think bats are helpful

   J no one has ever heard of bats

Name: _____ Date: _____

The Scoop on Sugar

Directions: Read this text and respond to the questions on pages 19–21.

1   Can you imagine eating 20 teaspoons of sugar? Does that sound gross? The typical American kid gets that much sugar each day.

2   A recent report said kids get about 16 percent of their calories from sugar that has been added to food. "It's too much," says Dr. David Katz. He's a nutrition expert at Yale University. "It's one of the major problems with our diet," he told TIME For Kids.

3   Some of that sugar comes from foods like candy, soda, and cereal. You expect them to be sweet. But much of the sugar that kids eat is hidden. Food companies add sugar to lots of things, from ketchup to crackers. "There are pasta sauces that have more added sugar than ice-cream toppings," says Katz.

4   As a result, people get used to eating very sweet foods. "If you soak taste buds in sugar all day long, they just get used to it," Katz says. "Everything needs to be highly sweetened to be satisfying."

Cut the Sugar

5   Most kids know that eating too much sugar is not healthy. Sugar can cause cavities. And filling up on sweets means not eating more nutritious foods. Some experts think that eating too much sugar can also lead to serious health problems.

6   Three scientists have called on the government to help people eat less sugar. They want to ban the sale of sugary drinks to kids. They want to keep sugary foods out of schools. And they want to add taxes to heavily sweetened foods. "We need to unsweeten our lives," Dr. Robert Lustig, one of the scientists, told TIME For Kids.

Name: _____   Date: _____

The Scoop on Sugar *(cont.)*

Expand Your Choices

7   We need food to live. It should help keep us healthy. Now we're learning our food may be doing the opposite. Perhaps someday the changes scientists want will happen. In the meantime, what can you do to cut down on extra sugar? Changing our eating habits isn't easy. We like the foods we like. The good news is, you don't have to give up your favorite cereal or soda completely. The key is to find balance.

8   First, look at the ingredients list on food packages. Packages may use different names for sugar. Ingredients that end in *ose* are sugars. Sucrose and fructose are two examples. The word *syrup* means that it's a sugar, too.

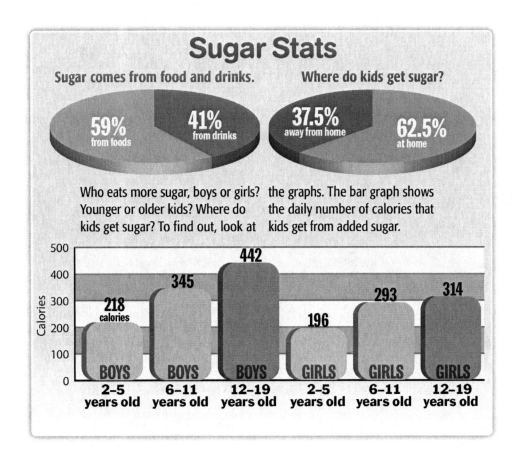

Sugar Stats

Sugar comes from food and drinks.

59% from foods   **41%** from drinks

Where do kids get sugar?

37.5% away from home   **62.5%** at home

Who eats more sugar, boys or girls? Younger or older kids? Where do kids get sugar? To find out, look at the graphs. The bar graph shows the daily number of calories that kids get from added sugar.

	BOYS 2–5 years old	BOYS 6–11 years old	BOYS 12–19 years old	GIRLS 2–5 years old	GIRLS 6–11 years old	GIRLS 12–19 years old
Calories	218 calories	345	442	196	293	314

GO ON

Name: _____ Date: _____

The Scoop on Sugar *(cont.)*

9 Second, try new things! Replace some of those sugary foods with ones that don't have added sugar. Expand your choices. You'll find lots of different foods that also taste great.

10 Dr. Lustig says to eat natural foods such as fresh fruits and vegetables. Stay away from processed foods. "Eat real food," he says. "Food that came out of the ground or animals that ate food that came out of the ground." Now that's food for thought.

Name: _____ Date: _____

The Scoop on Sugar *(cont.)*

Directions: Read each question carefully. Record the correct answer on your answer sheet.

1 The author most likely wrote this article to —

   A convince people to eat a balance of healthy foods and sugary foods

   B tell people to stop eating sugar

   C explain that only fruits and vegetables are healthy

   D amuse people with opinions from experts

2 Which sentence from the article supports the answer to number 1?

   F *First, look at the ingredients list on food packages.*

   G *Food companies add sugar to lots of things, from ketchup to crackers.*

   H *Stay away from processed foods.*

   J *Replace some of those sugary foods with ones that don't have added sugar.*

3 How much sugar does the average American kid eat daily?

   A 16 tablespoons

   B 16 teaspoons

   C 20 teaspoons

   D 20 tablespoons

GO ON ➡

Name: _____ Date: _____

The Scoop on Sugar (cont.)

4 Which sentence summarizes the author's main message?

    F Eating too much sugar is bad for us.

    G Food companies are trying to harm children.

    H The government needs to add taxes on sugary foods.

    J Crackers, ketchup, and pasta sauce are bad for us.

---

5 What is the meaning of <u>nutrition expert</u> in paragraph 2?

    A A person who does not like sugar

    B A person who knows which foods are good and bad for us

    C A scientist who studies sugar

    D A person who works for the government

---

6 Which of the following can be learned from the "Sugar Stats" graph?

    F Sugary foods do not always taste sweet

    G Which foods contain the most sugar

    H Most kids eat sugar away from home

    J Who is eating sugar at various ages

GO ON

Name: _____ Date: _____

The Scoop on Sugar (cont.)

7 Paragraphs 5 and 6 are mainly about —

    A the need to cut back on sugar

    B how sugar causes cavities

    C the diseases caused by sugar

    D what scientists study

---

8 Which of the following is **NOT** a word that means sugar?

    F Fructose

    G Sucrose

    H Calorie

    J Syrup

Name: _____ Date: _____

A Woman Up a Tree

Directions: Read this text and respond to the questions on pages 24–26.

1 Julia "Butterfly" Hill is a woman who lives her beliefs. Like real butterflies, Hill has spent a lot of time up in the air. For two years, she lived in the branches of a redwood tree. In 1997, Hill climbed the 200-foot-tall tree as a protest. She wanted to stop loggers from cutting down redwood trees in northern California. She said, "Here I can be the voice and face of this tree."

2 It was a tough two years for Hill. At last her sacrifice paid off. She came down after a lumber company said it wouldn't touch the 1,000-year-old giant.

3 Just a year later, the tree was in danger again. In 2000 someone cut deep into the tree's trunk with a chain saw. No one was ever caught. But the cut made the tree weak and unstable.

4 Experts fear it could be blown over by strong winter storms. Recently, Hill visited the tree, which she named Luna. She touched the 32-inch gash and said, "I feel this vicious attack on Luna as if the chain saw was going through me."

5 Hill feels strongly about the tree. When she came down from it after two years, she was sad: "I just felt like my heart was being ripped out." She added, "That tree was the best friend I've ever had." While on Luna, Hill lived in a 6-foot by 8-foot tree house. She had no shower. Friends sent up food in buckets. She cooked the food on a small gas-burning stove. She kept in shape by climbing the branches of the 18-story-high tree.

Julia "Butterfly" Hill checks the braces holding up the tree.

Shaun Walker/Eureka Times-Standard/AP

GO ON

51705—TIME For Kids: Practicing for STAAR Success   © *Shell Education*

Name: _____ Date: _____

A Woman Up a Tree *(cont.)*

6 Hill spent most of her time in the tree talking on a cell phone. For six to eight hours a day, she gave interviews. She explained what she was doing to school students. She got about 300 letters each week from people all over the world. Most mentioned how much Hill inspired them by helping Luna.

7 Luna survived the nasty cut. An emergency team put steel braces over the gash. They did this to support the tree. It looks like the tree will live. Hill belongs to an environmental group. It is called Circle of Life Foundation. It is working with experts to figure out how to save the tree permanently.

Experts reach around the giant tree to measure the damage.

Shaun Walker/Eureka Times-Standard/AP

GO ON

Name: _____ Date: _____

A Woman Up a Tree *(cont.)*

Directions: Read each question carefully. Record the correct answer on your answer sheet.

1   Why did Hill spend two years in the tree?

    A She wanted to save it from being cut down.

    B She liked being up off the ground.

    C She wished she could be a butterfly.

    D She was homeless.

2   Which statement by Hill tells why she stayed in the tree for so long?

    F "I feel this vicious attack on Luna as if the chain saw was going through me."

    G "Here I can be the voice and face of this tree."

    H "That tree was the best friend I've ever had."

    J "I just felt like my heart was being ripped out."

3   Why did Hill finally come down from the tree?

    A She wanted to live in a house.

    B Lumber companies promised not to cut it down.

    C She thought the tree was dead.

    D She did not like living outdoors.

51705—TIME For Kids: Practicing for STAAR Success

Name: _____ Date: _____

A Woman Up a Tree (cont.)

4   How do you think the author feels about saving Luna?

   F   The author believes it is silly.

   G   The author believes it is hopeless.

   H   The author believes Hill should focus on the other trees in the forest.

   J   The author believes that saving the tree is a good thing.

---

5   Read these sentences from paragraph 2.

> *It was a tough two years for Hill. At last her sacrifice paid off.*

What does the phrase <u>her sacrifice paid off</u> mean?

   A   She managed to protect the tree.

   B   She earned money for saving the tree.

   C   She paid money to save the tree.

   D   She changed her mind about saving the tree.

---

6   The photographs included in the article help the reader —

   F   visualize Hill's treehouse

   G   determine why Hill lived in the tree

   H   understand what the tree looks like

   J   recognize the people who damaged the tree

GO ON ➡

Name: _____ Date: _____

A Woman Up a Tree *(cont.)*

7 Which word is the best synonym for the word <u>vicious</u>?

    A Scary

    B Frightening

    C Mean

    D Unexpected

---

8 Which statement best summarizes the article?

    F Luna is an old tree. It is home to many animals and is 1,000 years old. Many people love Luna.

    G Julia Hill wanted to protect an old tree. She lived in the tree for two years to keep it from being cut down. Now experts are working to save the tree.

    H There are people in the world who do not like trees. They try to cut down even the oldest ones. They think trees are better used for other things.

    J Julie Hill loves a tree named Luna. She wants to be close to Luna all the time. She lived in the tree for two years. It is her best friend.

Name: _____ Date: _____

The Coral Reef Crisis

Directions: Read this text and respond to the questions on pages 29–31.

1   Under the clear blue sea, groups of ocean creatures live together in brightly colored structures. These underwater cities are called coral reefs. They have been around for millions of years.

2   But danger looms. Scientists are worried about the world's coral reefs. They have given a strong warning. Pollution and careless humans have wrecked more than a quarter of all reefs. If things don't improve soon, all the reefs may die in the next 20 years. That would put thousands of sea creatures at risk of dying out.

Precious Habitats

3   Coral seems like rock. It has a stone-like surface. But it is actually made up of tiny clear animals. They are coral polyps. Many are less than one inch wide. Millions of coral polyps stick together. They form colonies. They grow a hard shell. As these colonies grow bigger, they merge. They make big reefs. The bright color of coral comes from algae. Algae are tiny sea plants. Coral and algae depend on each other to live.

4   Coral may feel tough. Yet it's very delicate. Pollution has hurt many reefs. Bad fishing methods have also caused terrible harm. One problem is when people throw dynamite into the water. They do it to shock fish. It makes them easier to catch. But it blows up part of the reef.

5   The biggest threat is that oceans are getting warmer. Warm water causes coral to lose the algae that provide its food and color. This deadly process is called coral bleaching.

GO ON

Name: _____   Date: _____

The Coral Reef Crisis *(cont.)*

It's Time to Help

6   Scientists think that the reefs can still be saved. People must outlaw bad practices and control pollution. "The world's attitude must change," says scientist Clive Wilkinson. Maybe it already has. A group called the United Nations Foundation said it would give $10 million to help save the reefs. The money will be used to study reefs and teach people how to help.

Pollution has caused sea plants to strangle the reef in the photo on the left. Warm water has bleached the reef on the right.

Bob Cranston/Mo Young Productions

GO ON ➡

Name: _____   Date: _____

The Coral Reef Crisis

Directions: Read each question carefully. Record the correct answer on your answer sheet.

1   What might happen if ocean warming and pollution are not controlled?

   A Underwater cities may be formed.

   B There may be more pollution.

   C Coral polyps may stick together.

   D Most coral reefs may die in 20 years.

2   The author's purpose for writing this article is most likely —

   F to inform readers about ocean pollution

   G to teach readers about coral reefs

   H to tell readers about the troubles coral reefs face

   J to end fishing in the oceans

3   Which sentence from the article supports the author's main purpose?

   A *Scientists are worried about the world's coral reefs.*

   B *One problem is when people throw dynamite into the water.*

   C *Coral seems like rock.*

   D *These underwater cities are called coral reefs.*

GO ON

Name: _____ Date: _____

The Coral Reef Crisis *(cont.)*

4 What is the biggest threat to coral reefs?

   F Ocean water is getting warmer.

   G People throw dynamite into the water.

   H People pollute the oceans.

   J Bad fishing methods are used.

---

5 Which word best describes the tone of the article?

   A Fear

   B Danger

   C Concern

   D Excitement

---

6 What is the main reason the author includes the photos at the end of the article?

   F To show the dangers facing coral reefs

   G To show great places to go snorkeling

   H To provide more detail about coral colonies

   J To add pretty images to the article

Name: _____ Date: _____

The Coral Reef Crisis *(cont.)*

7 Read the diagram.

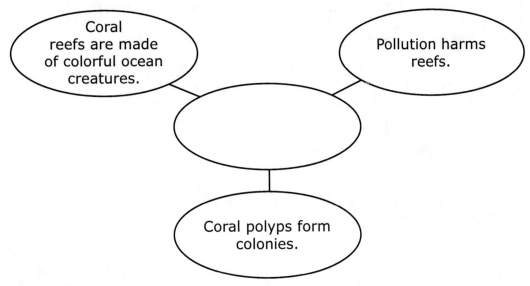

Which of the following correctly completes the diagram?

A Facts About Pollution

B Facts About Coral Reefs

C Facts About the Ocean

D Facts About Snorkeling

8 What is the best summary of this article?

F Coral reefs are amazing to see.

G People are purposely damaging coral reefs.

H Coral reefs are in danger, but can be saved.

J Scientists are very interested in coral polyp colonies.

STOP

Name: _____ Date: _____

Undersea Volcanoes

Directions: Read this text and respond to the questions on pages 34–36.

1   No one has ever seen some of the world's biggest volcanoes. Why? They are deep under the sea. You would have to dive down a mile and a half just to reach the tops! This string of underwater volcanoes is called the Mid-Ocean Ridge.

2   The Mid-Ocean Ridge is the biggest mountain range on our planet. It's more than 30,000 miles long. It is almost 500 miles wide. It has hundreds of mountains and volcanoes. They zigzag under the sea between the continents. They wind their way around the globe like the seam on a baseball. Nearly every day, at least one underwater volcano <u>erupts</u>.

These volcanic-island formations rise right out of the water.

GO ON ➡

Name: _____ Date: _____

Undersea Volcanoes (cont.)

3   This means that the bottom of the sea is always changing. Hot lava comes from deep inside the Earth. It pours out of the volcano. It spills onto the sea floor. As the lava cools, it forms rock. Layers of rocky lava pile up. Over millions of years, all that lava makes the sea floor expand. As the sea floor expands, it pushes the continents around. That is why a million years ago, the Earth looked very different than it does today. A million years from now, it will have changed again.

4   When volcanoes erupt underwater, they may form a mountain. This mountain may reach the surface of the sea. It forms a volcanic island. That's how Surtsey was created.

5   Surtsey first appeared in 1963. It is off the coast of Iceland. Iceland is an island nation. It is in the Atlantic Ocean. The erupting volcano had risen 300 feet from the bottom of the ocean. Icelanders named the new island after their god of fire.

6   For three and a half years, lava kept flowing. Surtsey grew and grew. At last the lava stopped in 1967. By then, the island was a mile wide and 560 feet high.

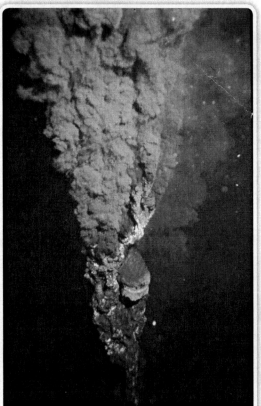

Woods Hole Oceanographic Institution

Each Hawaiian island began as an undersea volcano.

GO ON ➡

Name: _____ Date: _____

Undersea Volcanoes *(cont.)*

Directions: Read each question carefully. Record the correct answer on your answer sheet.

1   Why have people not seen some of the world's biggest volcanoes?

    A They are underwater.

    B They wind around the globe.

    C Hot lava comes out of them.

    D They are on islands.

---

2   The author compares the line of underwater volcanoes to —

    F a baseball

    G the seam on a baseball

    H layers of rocky lava

    J the surface of the sea

---

3   What is the final stage in the formation of a volcanic island?

    A Hot lava spills out and cools.

    B A volcano erupts underwater.

    C Lava expands the floor of the sea.

    D Lava builds up layers of rock.

Name: _____ Date: _____

Undersea Volcanoes (cont.)

4 What is the name of the largest mountain range on the planet?

F The Rocky Mountains

G The Iceland mountain range

H The Mid-Ocean Ridge

J The Undersea Volcano range

---

5 What is the meaning of the word <u>erupt</u>?

A Lava

B Burst

C Roar

D Flow

---

6 What can be inferred by the photo on page 33 and its caption?

F At one time, the Hawaiian Islands did not exist.

G It would be dangerous to live on the Hawaiian Islands.

H The Hawaiian Islands are huge.

J The Hawaiian Islands are far from the mainland of the United States.

GO ON

Name: _____ Date: _____

Undersea Volcanoes *(cont.)*

7 Which of the following describes the Mid-Ocean Ridge?

A It is more than 30,000 miles long.

B It does not have active volcanoes anymore.

C It is like a small mountain range.

D No one has ever seen it.

---

8 Which sentence best completes the chart about the formation of Surtsey?

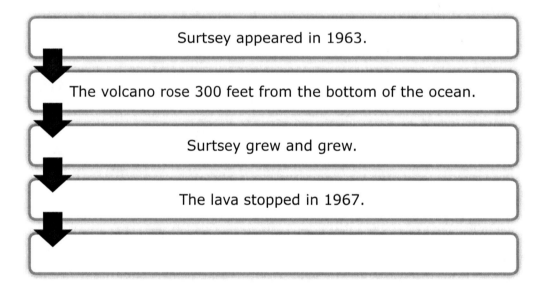

Surtsey appeared in 1963.

The volcano rose 300 feet from the bottom of the ocean.

Surtsey grew and grew.

The lava stopped in 1967.

F It is off the coast of Iceland.

G The island ended up being a mile wide and 560 feet high.

H Iceland is an island nation.

J For three and a half years, lava kept flowing.

STOP

Name: _____ Date: _____

She Gives Them Food for Thought

Directions: Read this text and respond to the questions on pages 38–40.

1   When it's time for science class, the kids at Martin Luther King Jr. Middle School start digging. They also start watering, weeding, and picking. Why? Their science class takes place in a garden.

2   The garden is in Berkeley, California. It is close to the students' school. It was started by a famous chef. Her name is Alice Waters. Waters helps the kids to grow carrots, strawberries, and other food. Everything in the garden is organic. That means it is grown without the use of harmful chemicals.

3   Waters runs a restaurant. She also wrote several cookbooks. She is known for using locally grown and organic foods. She started the garden so kids could learn about healthful eating. The students use the garden for more than science class. Math, art, and social studies lessons are also taught there.

4   Waters has a goal. She wants the kids to learn to prepare and eat healthful meals. Too many kids eat only fast food. Waters wants them to know what it's like to taste fresh, homegrown fruits and vegetables. It seems to be working.

5   "Every time I see the kids," Waters says, "I know the garden is a good idea."

Thomas Heinser, bottom: Daniel Dobers

GO ON ➡

Name: _____ Date: _____

She Gives Them Food for Thought (cont.)

Directions: Read each question carefully. Record the correct answer on your answer sheet.

1   What is unusual about the students' science class?

     A   It takes place at a restaurant.

     B   It takes place in a garden.

     C   It takes place in a classroom.

     D   They learn to eat healthy.

---

2   Alice Waters teaches the students —

     F   how to run a restaurant

     G   how to do well in school

     H   how to grow food

     J   how to set goals

---

3   Which of the following do the students **NOT** learn about in Waters' class?

     A   How to grow carrots, strawberries, and other food

     B   How to grow organic food

     C   Healthful eating

     D   How to run a restaurant

GO ON

Name: _____ Date: _____

She Gives Them Food for Thought *(cont.)*

4 The author wants to communicate that —

    F Waters is a successful chef

    G Waters likes children

    H Waters likes to cook

    J Waters is doing something new and different

---

5 What fact can be inferred from the article?

    A Waters does not like to pull weeds.

    B Waters wants to be a school teacher.

    C Waters does not think chemicals should be used on food.

    D Waters is an unhealthy person.

---

6 The message communicated by the photographs is that —

    F science is the students' favorite class

    G Waters is a cheerful person

    H Waters enjoys growing food in the garden

    J Waters works very hard as a chef

GO ON ➡

Name: _____ Date: _____

She Gives Them Food for Thought *(cont.)*

7   What is the meaning of the word <u>organic</u>?

    A   Grown for a restaurant

    B   Grown without chemicals

    C   Grown on a rooftop

    D   Grown by local gardeners

---

8   Complete the graphic organizer.

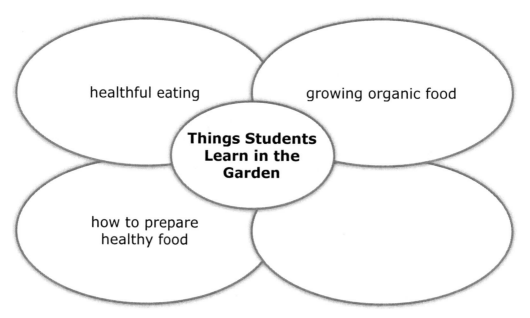

    F   Math, art, and social studies

    G   How to write cookbooks

    H   Physical education and music

    J   How to be chefs

Name: _____ Date: _____

For Sale: Rare and Stolen Pets

Directions: Read this text and respond to the questions on pages 43–45.

1 Animals are jammed into cages at a market in Mexico City. Green parrots and toucans squawk loudly. Many of these animals are rare or endangered. That means there are very few left in the wild. Still, they are being <u>snatched</u> and sold as pets.

2 Cats and dogs have been pets for thousands of years. Wild animals do not make good pets. They bite. They wreck homes and belongings. Even with loving owners, they die from not having the right food or environment.

Gerry Ellis/ENP Images

A chimpanzee sits in a cage after an animal thief was caught in Rwanda, a country in Africa. The chimp will be returned to its forest home.

GO ON ➤

Name: _____ Date: _____

For Sale: Rare and Stolen Pets *(cont.)*

3   Despite the risks, people want to own wild animals. So, all over the world, rare birds, reptiles, and monkeys are stolen from the wild. They are sneaked into pet markets. This illegal trade is worth billions of dollars. Some people will pay lots of money for a rare pet. For example, a scarlet macaw is a bird from Brazil. It can sell for $3,000.

4   Often poor people steal rare animals from the wild. They do it because they have no other income. They sell the animals to smugglers. The animals are taken to countries such as the United States.

5   Since it is against the law, the smugglers have to sneak the animals into the country. Some hide live birds in tennis ball cans. Others tape lizards under their shirts or put them into big suitcases with false bottoms.

6   The United States works with other countries to stop this trade. But there's just one sure way to end it. People must stop buying wild animals.

7   Jorge Picon works for the United States Fish and Wildlife Service. He works to keep rare animals out of pet stores. "Every shipment I see breaks my heart," he says. "These animals belong in the wild."

Name: _____ Date: _____

For Sale: Rare and Stolen Pets *(cont.)*

Directions: Read each question carefully. Record the correct answer on your answer sheet.

1   What is a synonym for the word <u>snatched</u> as used in paragraph 1?

    A Abused

    B Adopted

    C Collected

    D Stolen

---

2   Which sentence from the article helps the reader understand the meaning of the word <u>snatched</u>?

    F *Many of these animals are rare or endangered.*

    G *Wild animals do not make good pets.*

    H *Often poor people steal rare animals from the wild.*

    J *They sell the animals to smugglers.*

---

3   Why is it against the law to sell rare pets?

    A They destroy homes.

    B They are endangered.

    C They cost too much.

    D They bite people.

GO ON ➡

Name: _____ Date: _____

For Sale: Rare and Stolen Pets *(cont.)*

4 What is the overall message of the article?

F Poor people need another way to earn money.

G Macaws are almost extinct.

H Don't buy rare and endangered animals for pets.

J People should not own pets.

---

5 According to the article, what would be the effect if no one bought rare animals?

A They would no longer be stolen and smuggled.

B Pet stores would go out of business.

C Poor people would starve.

D The animals would die in the wild.

---

6 What can be inferred from the photograph on page 41 and its caption?

F The chimp will be free.

G The chimp is going to be sold.

H The chimp will be taken far from home.

J The chimp will be owned as a pet.

Name: _____ Date: _____

For Sale: Rare and Stolen Pets *(cont.)*

7 With which statement would the author most likely agree?

   A Exotic pets need to have loving owners.

   B Wild animals do not make good pets.

   C Poor people need to make money by selling rare animals.

   D The United States Fish and Wildlife Service should humanely help bring exotic animals into the country.

---

8 Which paragraph offers a solution for the problem?

   F Paragraph 2

   G Paragraph 4

   H Paragraph 5

   J Paragraph 6

Name: _____ Date: _____

Threads of Kindness

Directions: Read this text and respond to the questions on pages 47–49.

1 More than 30 years ago, Tran Duyen Hai went for a walk. Tran lives in Hanoi. It is the capital city of Vietnam. It is a country in Southeast Asia. Tran's walk that day took him around the shore of a large lake. He saw two teenage girls sitting by the path. They were crying.

2 "They looked so miserable," he says. "I went over to talk to them."

3 As he got nearer, he noticed both girls were disabled. They couldn't walk.

4 "They told me they'd been to a government job-training center but had been turned away."

5 A lightbulb went on in Tran's mind. His job was training people to work in a <u>garment factory</u>. It was work that someone could do sitting down. He offered to give the girls free sewing lessons. They agreed. To Tran's surprise, seven disabled girls showed up for the first lesson. A month later, Tran had 12 students, then 25. He retired from his job. He wanted to spend all his time teaching disabled kids.

Tran teaches disabled teenagers to sew.

Peter Charlesworth/On Asia Images

6 Ever since, Tran has run a center for disabled children. He started the center with $1,500 of his own savings. Now he gets help from his family and from charities. He has helped to find jobs for thousands of teenagers.

7 Do Thi Toan is one of Tran's former students. She used to worry about finding a good job. Today, she earns enough to send some money to her family. She and all his other students are very happy that Tran took that walk around the lake.

Name: _____   Date: _____

Threads of Kindness *(cont.)*

Directions: Read each question carefully. Record the correct answer on your answer sheet.

1 What is a <u>garment factory</u>?

    A A company where clothes are made

    B A company that teaches people how to sew

    C A place that helps people who cannot walk

    D A government training center

_____

2 How does teaching the teenagers to sew help them?

    F It gives them something to do.

    G It makes them smile.

    H They are able to get jobs.

    J They can make their own clothes.

_____

3 The main reason that Do Thi Toan is happy about learning to sew is because —

    A she can sew sitting down

    B she now has a job and can earn money

    C she is not able to walk

    D she gets help from charities

GO ON ➡

Name: _____ Date: _____

Threads of Kindness *(cont.)*

4   Where does Tran go for a walk?

   F   Near the garment factory

   G   Around a lake

   H   Near a school

   J   By a home for disabled girls

---

5   What is the author's main message?

   A   Sewing is fun.

   B   More people should learn how to sew.

   C   It is kind to talk to someone who is crying.

   D   It is wonderful to help people.

---

6   What does the reader learn from the photograph and caption?

   F   Tran teaches teenagers to sew in a classroom.

   G   Tran likes to make his own clothes.

   H   The girls make a lot of money.

   J   Tran is a nice man.

GO ON

Name: _____ Date: _____

Threads of Kindness *(cont.)*

7 Which word best describes Tran?

  A Funny

  B Hyperactive

  C Thoughtful

  D Unhappy

---

8 Look at the diagram below.

Which of the following completes the diagram?

  F The girls were not allowed to attend a government job-training program.

  G The girls were not able to get wheelchairs to help them.

  H The girls did not have friends.

  J The girls had lost their families.

Name: _____ Date: _____

The Long Trail

from *The Call of the Wild* by Jack London

Directions: Read this story and respond to the questions on pages 51–53.

1   Buck was tired, more tired than he ever thought he could be. He and the other dogs had been on the trail for 30 days. They were hauling the sled from the town of Dawson to the town of Skagway in Alaska. That was more than 400 miles across the solidly frozen Yukon.

2   The Yukon was filled with optimistic men who had come to look for gold and seek their fortune. Most of them had wives or sweethearts back home. All of those loved ones wrote letters. So a pile of mail arrived by ship at Skagway. It had to be hauled by sled over the mountains to Dawson. Then all the answering letters had to be hauled back.

3   The wind was bitingly cold. The snow and ice hurt Buck's paws. It was even harder on the other dogs, who were smaller. The one called Sol-leks was limping and so was Pike. Dub's shoulder was aching painfully. All of them had aching paws.

4   There was no spring left in them; their feet fell heavily on the trail. There was nothing the matter with the dogs except that they were dead tired. Every muscle, every fiber, every cell was tired, dead tired.

5   "Mush on, poor sore feet!" the driver called. The men were tired, too. But that mountain of mail had to be delivered. The driver snapped his whip. "Mush on!" he shouted.

6   Buck lowered his head and strained against the harness. The sled moved on over the cold, stinging snow.

Andrew Wenzel/Master File

GO ON

Name: _____ Date: _____

The Long Trail *(cont.)*

Directions: Read each question carefully. Record the correct answer on your answer sheet.

1   Who or what is Buck?

   A A sled driver

   B A fortune seeker

   C A mailman

   D A dog

---

2   Which sentence gives evidence to support who or what Buck is?

   F *Most of them had wives or sweethearts back home.*

   G *The snow and ice hurt Buck's paws.*

   H *'Mush on, poor sore feet!' the driver called.*

   J *There was nothing the matter with the dogs except that they were dead tired.*

---

3   What can the reader infer will happen next?

   A Buck will stop for a long rest.

   B Buck and the other dogs will keep going even though they are tired.

   C The sled driver will decide not to continue on.

   D The dogs will refuse to go any farther.

GO ON

Name: _____ Date: _____

The Long Trail *(cont.)*

4 In paragraph 2, the word <u>optimistic</u> means —

   F hardworking

   G rich

   H hopeful

   J strong

---

5 What is the main message that the author communicates?

   A Surviving in the Yukon is not easy.

   B It is hard for people to be separated from loved ones.

   C There are lots of mountains in the Yukon.

   D Sled dogs make good pets.

---

6 The purpose of the photograph is most likely —

   F to show how sled dogs work

   G to show that sled dogs are beautiful

   H to show how much fun it is to ride a dogsled

   J to show that Alaska is snowy

GO ON

Name: _____ Date: _____

The Long Trail *(cont.)*

7 Which best completes the diagram?

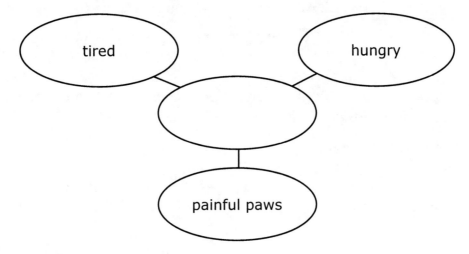

A Sled Driver's feelings

B Yukon Trails

C Dogs' Harnesses

D Dogs' Conditions

---

8 Who is the narrator of the passage?

F Buck

G Dawson

H A sled driver

J An outside observer

Name: _____ Date: _____

Paul Bunyan

Directions: Read this story and respond to the questions on pages 55–57.

1 Five storks delivered a huge baby to the Bunyans. They lived in Bangor, Maine. The parents named him Paul.

2 To fill Paul's bottle, the Bunyans milked 24 cows from sunrise to sunset. For breakfast, Paul ate 10 barrels of porridge.

3 Paul destroyed forests as he rolled around in his sleep. So his parents built a raft and let the napping baby float in the ocean. But Paul turned over and caused a tidal wave. The Bunyans realized the eastern United States was too small for Paul. They moved to Minnesota.

4 One day when he was a young man, Paul saw a tiny blue ox struggling to climb a snowdrift. Paul took the ox home and warmed him by the fire. Even once the ox warmed up, it remained blue. Paul decided to call him Babe the Blue Ox.

5 Babe grew to <u>unreal proportions</u>. It took a whole day for a bird to fly from one of his horns to the other! Babe ate 30 bales of hay just as a snack.

Matt Collins for Time For Kids

6 Babe helped Paul with his job as a lumberjack. They left their mark wherever they roamed. As they stomped around Minnesota, they made giant footprints in the ground. Rain filled their tracks. And that is how the state's famous 10,000 lakes were formed.

GO ON

Name: _____ Date: _____

Paul Bunyan *(cont.)*

Directions: Read each question carefully. Record the correct answer on your answer sheet.

1   Which detail shows just how much Paul's parents are willing to do for him?

   A They get him an ox.

   B They move to Minnesota so he can have more space.

   C They ask storks for a baby.

   D They want him to be a lumberjack.

2   What genre is the Paul Bunyan story?

   F A fable

   G A mystery

   H A nursery rhyme

   J A folktale

3   How are Paul and Babe similar?

   A They are both from Bangor, Maine.

   B They are both very big.

   C They both drink a lot of milk.

   D They both move to Minnesota.

GO ON

Name: _____ Date: _____

Paul Bunyan *(cont.)*

4 What does it mean that Babe grew to <u>unreal proportions</u>?

   F Babe was very tiny.

   G Babe causes a tidal wave when he walks.

   H Babe eats a lot of food.

   J Babe grows so large it is hard to imagine.

---

5 Which sentence describes Babe's size?

   A *Even once the ox warmed up, it remained blue.*

   B *Babe helped Paul with his job as a lumberjack.*

   C *It took a whole day for a bird to fly from one of his horns to the other.*

   D *They left their mark wherever they roamed.*

---

6 The purpose of the illustration is most likely —

   F to show that Paul's family lives in a log cabin

   G to show that Babe is Paul's friend

   H to show how much bigger Paul and Babe are compared to everything else

   J to show that Paul likes being a lumberjack

Name: _____ Date: _____

Paul Bunyan *(cont.)*

7 Which detail from the story provides evidence that it is fictional?

   A Paul cut down trees.

   B An ox helped Paul work.

   C Paul ate 10 barrels of porridge for breakfast.

   D Paul had a family.

---

8 Which of the following characteristics of a baby is fictional?

   F Drinks milk

   G Delivered by a stork

   H Takes naps

   J Has parents

Name: _____ Date: _____

Go Fly a Kite!

Directions: Read this story and respond to the questions on pages 60–62.

1 I was just leaving my house when my mother called out to me. "Ezra, did you take your key with you?" My mother held out the key in her hand. I grabbed it, and she said sternly, "A ten-year-old boy must not be locked out of his house."

2 I had a good reason to forget my key. I was about to see Philadelphia's greatest citizen, Benjamin Franklin. Of course, Ben was not expecting me on this June day in 1752. Nor was his son, William. Neither one knew me, but I knew of them.

3 By accident, I had heard William tell a shopkeeper that he and his father were going to fly a kite this day. I knew he was up to something, and I wanted to watch the genius at work. I knew where Ben Franklin lived—everyone in Philadelphia did. So I waited outside his house. Soon, father and son left the house carrying some large objects.

David Wenzel

Name: _____ Date: _____

Go Fly a Kite! *(cont.)*

4   I followed them to a farm right outside the city and hid behind a tree. Ben and William watched the sky, and as storm clouds gathered, Ben said, "Let's get ready."

5   Ben attached a string to the kite. Then he looked around for something. "Where is the key, William?" he asked. His son looked in his pockets but found no key.

6   "I cannot do the experiment without a key," said Ben. "We might as well go home."

7   At that moment, I leaped from behind the tree. "Mr. Franklin, I have a key." I held up the key to my house.

8   I glowed with pride when Ben exclaimed, "You have saved the day, young man!" I handed him the key, and he tied it near the end of the string. Next, he attached a metal wire to the key, which led to a glass jar.

9   Ben said to me, "I am performing an experiment to see if lightning is made of electricity. If it is, the electricity will be drawn from the kite to the metal key. Then it will flow into this special jar that collects electricity."

10 William got the kite flying, as rain began to fall. Holding the kite string, Ben led us into a nearby barn to stay dry. Before long, we saw a flash of lightning. Did his experiment work? Ben put his hand near the key. An electric spark jumped from the key to his fingers.

11 "We have done it!" he exclaimed. "We proved that lightning is made of electricity. And I could not have done it without you," he said to me.

12 When I got home, I realized I had left my key with Ben. I had helped <u>unlock a secret of nature</u>—but I couldn't unlock my front door!

GO ON

Name: _____ Date: _____

Go Fly a Kite!

Directions: Read each question carefully. Record the correct answer on your answer sheet.

1   What does the phrase <u>unlock a secret of nature</u> from paragraph 12 mean?

    A Use a key to open a door

    B Discover something new about the world

    C Fly a kite in a storm

    D Keep a secret you have been told

---

2   How well-known is Ben Franklin in 1752?

    F He is not known by many people.

    G No one knows who he is.

    H The people who live nearby know him.

    J Everybody in the city knows him.

---

3   Which word would best describe Ben?

    A Genius

    B Lazy

    C Impatient

    D Rich

GO ON

Name: _____ Date: _____

Go Fly a Kite! *(cont.)*

4 Which sentence represents the climax of the story?

F *William got the kite flying, as rain began to fall.*

G *Ben said to me, "I am performing an experiment to see if lightning is made of electricity."*

H *An electric spark jumped from the key to his fingers.*

J *When I got home, I realized I had left my key with Ben.*

---

5 The author's purpose in writing this story is most likely —

A to let people know that Ben had a son

B to show that Ben was a scientist

C to tell a famous story from a different point of view

D to let people know that Ben took risks

---

6 What does the reader learn from the illustration?

F How men and boys dressed at that time

G That they all ended up soaking wet

H How Ezra got in trouble for losing his key

J That Ben enjoyed flying kites daily

GO ON

Go Fly a Kite! *(cont.)*

7 Which two words describe how Ezra felt when he helped Ben with the experiment and how he felt when he got home?

   A Excited and tired

   B Curious and happy

   C Ashamed and silly

   D Proud and foolish

---

8 How does Ezra feel about Ben Franklin?

   F Ezra admires Ben.

   G Ezra is afraid of Ben.

   H Ezra thinks of Ben as a father.

   J Ezra knows nothing about Ben.

Name: _____ Date: _____

A Bedouin Tale

Directions: Read this story and respond to the questions on pages 65–67.

1   Bedouins are nomads who live in the deserts of Arabia. A long time ago, there was a Bedouin leader named Abu Yusef. He was known for his courage and fairness. For many years, he helped keep peace in the region. He stopped the many tribes from fighting one another. Then, one day, Abu Yusef became very ill. His three sons, Yusef, Zaid, and Omar, argued about who should take charge if their father died.

2   "I am the eldest, and it's only fair that I should be in power," Yusef said to the men of the tribe. Omar, the youngest son, said that since he was his father's favorite, he would make the best leader. The middle brother, Zaid, shouted, "It's clear that I should be the one in charge."

Drew Willis for Time For Kids

3   Abu Yusef heard the fighting among his sons. He felt very upset. He called his children to his bedside. "My beloved sons, you must prove your strength to me," he said. "I want each of you to bring me the largest tree branch you can find." When they returned, Abu Yusef instructed each of them to break his branch.

4   "I can easily break this," said Yusef. And in one quick snap, it was broken. Abu Yusef then asked Zaid if he could do the same. Zaid broke an even larger branch. Omar did, too.

GO ON ➡

Name: _____ Date: _____

A Bedouin Tale *(cont.)*

5   But Abu Yusef did not look satisfied. He asked his sons to gather the broken branches and tie them all together. "Can one of you break all of these together?" he asked.

6   Each son took a turn. Each tried hard but without success.

7   "You see, my sons, each stick is easy to break on its own, but together, they are stronger. The same is true for you," Abu Yusef said.

8   The brothers understood their father's message: Alone, each son was weak, but together, they were strong.

Name: _____ Date: _____

A Bedouin Tale *(cont.)*

Directions: Read each question carefully. Record the correct answer on your answer sheet.

1   What is the purpose of this story?

   A   To make people laugh

   B   To teach a lesson

   C   To entertain

   D   To provide factual information

---

2   What word best describes Abu Yusef?

   F   Mean

   G   Furious

   H   Caring

   J   Happy

---

3   Which paragraph of the story communicates a message to the reader?

   A   Paragraph 2

   B   Paragraph 3

   C   Paragraph 6

   D   Paragraph 8

GO ON

Name: _____ Date: _____

A Bedouin Tale *(cont.)*

4 Why is including the dialogue important to understanding the story?

   F It helps the reader to understand that the sons are selfish.

   G It helps the reader to understand that the father wants the sons to work together.

   H It helps the reader to understand how the father works with other people.

   J It helps the reader to understand Abu Yusef's life.

---

5 Which sentence from the story provides evidence that the sons were selfish?

   A *Each tried hard but without success.*

   B *His three sons, Yusef, Zaid, and Omar, argued about who should take charge if their father died.*

   C *You see, my sons, each stick is easy to break on its own, but together, they are stronger.*

   D *But Abu Yusef did not look satisfied.*

---

6 What is the purpose of the illustration on page 63?

   F To show how the men dressed

   G To show that the father was unhappy with his sons

   H To show how big the branches were

   J To show how hard the brothers tried to prove their strength

Name: _____ Date: _____

A Bedouin Tale *(cont.)*

7 What is the moral of the story?

  A Sons should be good to their fathers.

  B People are stronger when they work together.

  C Families should not fight.

  D Hard work is rewarding.

---

8 Look at the diagram.

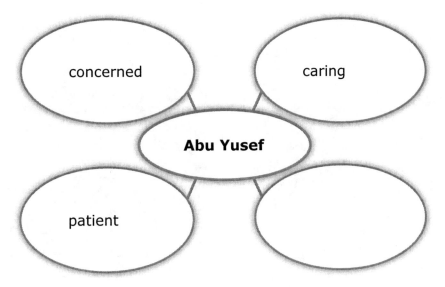

Complete the diagram with one of the words below.

  F Mean

  G Silly

  H Wise

  J Unforgiving

STOP

Name: _____ Date: _____

The Lion and the Wild Boar

Directions: Read this story and respond to the questions on pages 69–71.

1   One hot day a lion and a wild boar arrived at a pond at the same moment. "I got here first—wait your turn!" cried the wild boar. He blocked the lion's path.

2   "I am the king of all the beasts," roared the lion. "You should wait for me. I shouldn't have to drink water muddied by your hooves."

3   This angered the wild boar, and he attacked the lion, jabbing him with his sharp tusks. The lion grabbed the wild boar's throat with his teeth and would not let go. The brutal sun beat down on the thirsty pair until at last they both backed away from each other. Panting with exhaustion, they moved to opposite sides of the pond. While he rested, the lion looked up and noticed a group of buzzards clustered on a rock ledge, watching and waiting.

4   "Look up there," he said to the wild boar. "Those buzzards will eat whoever loses our battle. It doesn't matter to them whether it is me or you; they will pick clean the bones."

5   The wild boar looked at the birds. Then the lion and the wild boar looked at one another. "Let's stop fighting," they said at the same time.

6   The wild boar said, "Besides, there is plenty of water for us both." The lion added, "Drinking muddy water is better than being a buzzard's next meal."

7   Moral: Enemies will unite against a common enemy.

Name: _____ Date: _____

The Lion and the Wild Boar (cont.)

Directions: Read each question carefully. Record the correct answer on your answer sheet.

1 What will happen if the wild boar and the lion do not work out their differences?

    A They will fight until one dies.

    B They will go home.

    C They will scare away the buzzards.

    D They will make friends with the buzzards.

---

2 Which statement best expresses the theme of the story?

    F Fighting is bad.

    G Lions and wild boars cannot be friends.

    H Sometimes we have good reason to work with those we do not like.

    J Sometimes animals can become friends.

---

3 Which sentence from the text illustrates the theme?

    A *Enemies will unite against a common enemy.*

    B *The wild boar said, "Besides, there is plenty of water for us both."*

    C *Drinking muddy water is better than being a buzzard's next meal.*

    D *It doesn't matter to them whether it is me or you; they will pick clean the bones.*

GO ON ➡

Name: _____ Date: _____

The Lion and the Wild Boar *(cont.)*

4 Read this dictionary entry for the word <u>unite</u>.

> **unite** \u-nite\ *verb*
> **1.** to join into a single unit
> **2.** to stick together
> **3.** to link in a legal bond
> **4.** to combine by adhesion or mixture

Which meaning of <u>unite</u> is used in the last sentence?

F Meaning 1

G Meaning 2

H Meaning 3

J Meaning 4

---

5 Which sentence states the turning point in the story?

A The boar attacked the lion.

B They moved to opposite sides of the pond.

C The boar blocked the path.

D The boar and lion realized the buzzards would win in the end.

---

6 The lion and wild boar modify their original stances because —

F they change their opinions about each other

G they decide to be friends

H they do not want to be eaten by the buzzards

J they want to make friends with the buzzards

GO ON ▶

Name: _____ Date: _____

The Lion and the Wild Boar *(cont.)*

7   The lion thought he should drink first because —

   A he got there first

   B he wanted to drink before the boar made the water dirty

   C he did not like to drink while others were watching

   D he did not want to get his paws wet

---

8   How are the lion and the boar similar?

   F They are both king of the beasts.

   G They both have tusks.

   H They are both thirsty.

   J They are both unselfish.

Name: _____ Date: _____

Racing a Tornado

Directions: Read this story and respond to the questions on pages 74–76.

1   If we had known what was going to happen, we never would have gotten on our bikes. But it seemed like a perfect day for a long bike ride. Maria and I set out at 7 A.M. and didn't stop for lunch until noon. We sat under an oak tree and had a picnic. That's when the sky began to change and we began to worry.

2   In the distance, a towering bank of dark clouds appeared. We looked at each other. There was no way we could avoid that storm. What could we do?

The car sped away from the tornado as it came closer and closer.

GO ON

Name: _____ Date: _____

Racing a Tornado *(cont.)*

3   The weather quickly got worse. The sky was very dark, not like daytime at all. Trees were bending in the wind. Suddenly, a blue car pulled up alongside our bikes. The woman at the wheel rolled down the side window and shouted, "Get in!" The driver looked as frightened as we felt. We abandoned our bikes in the ditch and jumped into the car just as colossal chunks of hail began to fall.

4   The car sped away with hailstones the size of golf balls bouncing off the hood. Maria and I looked back at the black sky. Maria screamed and pointed, "There's a tornado!"

5   The black, twisting funnel seemed to be chasing us. It certainly was getting closer and closer. I was terrified. How could we outrun that monster?

6   "There's an overpass ahead," the driver said. "We'll use it for cover."

7   She brought the car to a stop under the bridge, and we all ran up the embankment. The woman yelled to us to lie flat. We squeezed down behind the concrete part of the structure, and not a minute too soon. A roaring like a freight train passed over us. Then, suddenly, it was over. We had survived—barely. That was a race we didn't ever want to run again!

GO ON

Name: _____ Date: _____

Racing a Tornado (cont.)

Directions: Read each question carefully. Record the correct answer on your answer sheet.

1   What is the tone of the text?

   A Excitement

   B Joy

   C Fear

   D Anger

2   Which sentence provides evidence of the text's tone?

   F *Trees were bending in the wind.*

   G *The driver looked as frightened as we felt.*

   H *The woman yelled to us to lie flat.*

   J *How could we outrun that monster?*

3   What are the two purposes of the photo and caption?

1. To show just how close the tornado was
2. To show the size of the tornado
3. To show the size of the hail
4. To show the area where the kids live

   A 1 and 2

   B 2 and 3

   C 3 and 4

   D 1 and 4

Name: _____   Date: _____

Racing a Tornado *(cont.)*

4   The genre of this story is —

   F   mystery

   G   fairy tale

   H   comedy

   J   suspense

---

5   Which is a synonym for the word <u>colossal</u> as used in paragraph 3?

   A   Sharp

   B   Cold

   C   Huge

   D   Interesting

---

6   Which example of dialogue expresses a command?

   F   *Maria screamed and pointed, "There's a tornado!"*

   G   *The woman at the wheel rolled down the side window and shouted, "Get in!"*

   H   *"There's an overpass ahead," the driver said.*

   J   *"We'll use it for cover."*

GO ON ➡

Name: _____ Date: _____

Racing a Tornado *(cont.)*

7 Read this sentence from paragraph 5.

> *How could we outrun this monster?*

This sentence helps the reader know that —

A the woman's car was slow

B the tornado had legs

C the kids lived far away

D the tornado was huge

---

8 Look at the diagram.

Which of the following completes the diagram?

F They saw huge hailstones.

G They outran the tornado.

H They jumped into a woman's car.

J The sky was dark.

Name: _____ Date: _____

The Treasure Hunt

Directions: Read this story and respond to the questions on pages 79–81.

1   Alex and Emma went walking on the beach. Emma pointed to something the tide had washed up on the shore.

2   Alex picked up the object. It was a glass bottle sealed tightly with a cork. There was something inside the bottle. Alex tried to pull out the cork, but it wouldn't budge. Emma grabbed it from him and managed to twist the cork out. She saw a paper in the bottle and pulled it out. She unfolded the paper. At the top were these words: "FOLLOW THE CLUES TO FIND A GREAT TREASURE!" Under this message was a set of clues.

3   Alex howled in excitement, "If we follow the clues, we'll find money or gold or diamonds!" They looked at the first number. The direction said: "It's where the money is."

4   "The place with money could be the bank," said Emma.

5   "Maybe," said Alex. He didn't like to admit his sister had good ideas. "Well, we can go there just in case."

6   Ten minutes later, they stood in front of the Sunshine Bank. There was lots of money inside, but it belonged to other people. There didn't seem to be any money hidden outside.

7   The clue for number two said, "Go two blocks north and one block west." The kids followed the directions and ended up at City Hall. They found nothing.

8   Clue three took them three blocks west to Paws Pet Store. Inside were sleepy kittens and puppies. A parrot squawked, "I dig it! I dig it!" The kids thought it might be a clue. "But dig where?" Alex asked the parrot. The parrot didn't answer. The store owner gave them a funny look.

9   The last clue said to go five blocks north and three blocks east. The pair ran the rest of the way. Gasping for breath, they stopped in front of the public library.

GO ON

Name: _____ Date: _____

The Treasure Hunt (cont.)

10 "What?" exclaimed Alex, disappointed. "There's no treasure here—just a lot of books."

11 "Let's go inside anyway," said Emma.

12 In the main room, the two looked at the clues again. What did *423.1 ref.* mean?

13 Emma walked up to the librarian and asked if she knew what it meant.

14 The librarian smiled and said, "Yes. It is a number in the Dewey Decimal System. Each nonfiction book has a Dewey Decimal number on its spine based on what type of book it is. That lets people easily find it on the shelves. The books are kept in numerical order. So go to the reference section and look until you find that number on the book's spine."

David Coulson

15 It didn't take Alex and Emma long to find a book that had 423.1 ref. on its spine. It was a dictionary!

16 "I don't get it!" said Alex unhappily. "This isn't a treasure. It's just an old book!"

17 Emma was silent for a moment. Then she said, "All the words in a language are in a dictionary. It helps us read, write, and speak. Without words, we couldn't say what we think and feel. We couldn't create ideas. Words let us move forward together. Look at how much we used words in this treasure hunt. This is a treasure after all!"

GO ON ➡

Name: _____ Date: _____

The Treasure Hunt (cont.)

Directions: Read each question carefully. Record the correct answer on your answer sheet.

1 Which two words best describe Emma?

> **1.** Disappointed
>
> **2.** Hopeful
>
> **3.** Careless
>
> **4.** Smart

A 1 and 3

B 2 and 4

C 3 and 4

D 1 and 4

---

2 How does Alex feel when they reach the library?

F Tired

G Excited

H Nervous

J Confused

---

3 Which sentence from the text provides evidence for the way Alex feels when he reaches the library?

A *Clue three took them three blocks west to Paws Pet Store.*

B *At the top were these words: "FOLLOW THE CLUES TO FIND A GREAT TREASURE!"*

C *A parrot squawked, "I dig it! I dig it!"*

D *"There's no treasure here—just a lot of books."*

GO ON

Name: _____ Date: _____

The Treasure Hunt *(cont.)*

4   Alex and Emma are most confused when they —

   F   find the bottle

   G   get to the bank

   H   are at the library

   J   discover that words are a treasure

---

5   What is one message the author communicates?

   A   There are different kinds of treasures.

   B   Looking for treasure is fun.

   C   People should work together.

   D   Librarians are helpful.

---

6   The purpose of the illustration is likely —

   F   to show that the library is very large

   G   to show that Alex is upset to get a book as a treasure

   H   to show that they tell the librarian that they found the treasure

   J   to show the number of clues the children follow

Name: _____ Date: _____

The Treasure Hunt *(cont.)*

7   Which of the following does **not** explain how words are a treasure?

   A   We use words to express feelings.

   B   We use words to share ideas.

   C   Words are in books.

   D   Words help us work together.

---

8   Look at the flow chart.

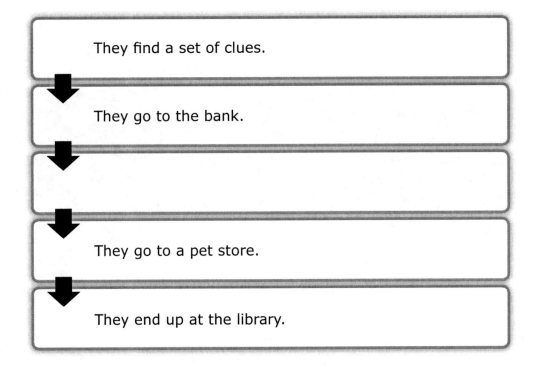

They find a set of clues.

They go to the bank.

They go to a pet store.

They end up at the library.

Which of the following completes the diagram?

   F   They find some books.

   G   They walk to City Hall.

   H   They talk to a parrot.

   J   They talk to a librarian.

Name: _____ Date: _____

It's a Dog's Life

Directions: Read this story and respond to the questions on pages 84–86.

1 "C'mon Butch, get the ball." Andy threw the ball and Butch raced across the yard. The dog caught the ball in his mouth, ran back to Andy, and dropped it at his feet. Ten minutes later, Andy said, "I know you love this game, but it's time to stop." Butch looked like he was smiling.

2 "I wish I knew what you're thinking, Butch," said Andy.

3 The next morning, Andy felt something wet. It was Butch licking his face. Suddenly, Andy heard, "I have to go out. Hurry up!"

4 Andy looked around but only Butch was in the room.

5 "Andy is so lazy."

6 Andy sat up in bed. "Who said that?"

7 "I'll try licking him again."

8 As Butch began to lick Andy, Andy jumped back. He thought, *I'm hearing things in my head, but there's no one around...except Butch.* "If I don't go outside right away, there's going to be an accident inside."

9 Andy was hearing Butch's thoughts! "Can you understand me?" Andy said aloud.

10 "Does he think I can talk?" Andy heard Butch think.

11 Andy was shocked and excited. Who could he tell about this? People would think he was nuts. "So, uh, Butch, you want to go outside?" asked Andy.

Kelly Kennedy

GO ON

Name: _____ Date: _____

It's a Dog's Life *(cont.)*

12 "I thought you'd never ask," thought Butch.

13 Outside, Andy picked up a ball and tossed it. "Fetch it, Butch!"

14 "Doesn't he ever get tired of this game? I know I do."

15 Andy was surprised; he'd been certain that Butch loved this game.

16 "Let's go for a walk, Butch." Andy put a leash on Butch. At the dog park, Andy unhooked the leash to let Butch play with other dogs. In the distance, he could pick up some of Butch's thoughts: "Andy is okay for a human," he told one of the other pooches.

17 "And I thought he really loved me," Andy thought, feeling a bit discouraged.

18 Later, at dinner, Andy put out a bowl of dog food. "Hey, Butch! Come and get it."

19 "Same old stuff, day after day. I want human food."

20 Andy and his family were eating at the kitchen table. He heard Butch think, "I smell steak—that's my favorite!" A second later, Butch was sitting next to Andy, staring at the steaks.

21 "No, Butch!" yelled Andy's mother. "Get down!"

22 "They won't even give me a taste? They're so selfish." Butch jumped up on the table, grabbed a steak, and ran out of the dining room.

23 Andy found Butch, curled up in his favorite spot. He stopped to hear his dog's thoughts:

24 "I play with them, walk with them, let them pet me, guard their house. And then they get upset over a piece of meat. It's not easy being a dog."

GO ON ➡

Name: _____ Date: _____

It's a Dog's Life (cont.)

Directions: Read each question carefully. Record the correct answer on your answer sheet.

1 Read the sentences below.

> **1.** He thinks Butch really loves him.
>
> **2.** He can hear Butch's thoughts.
>
> **3.** He finds out that Butch wants to eat steak.
>
> **4.** He learns that Butch doesn't like playing fetch.

Which two things surprise Andy the most?

A Statements 1 and 2

B Statements 1 and 3

C Statements 2 and 3

D Statements 2 and 4

2 How does Butch feel about playing fetch?

F He wants to play it all day.

G He would rather play fetch with other dogs.

H It is his favorite game.

J He only wants to play for a short time.

3 Which quotation from the story provides evidence for how Butch feels about playing fetch?

A "So, uh, Butch, you want to go outside?"

B "Doesn't he ever get tired of this game? I know I do."

C "Fetch it, Butch!"

D "Let's go for a walk, Butch."

Name: _____ Date: _____

It's a Dog's Life *(cont.)*

4   In the story, what is the meaning of the word <u>nuts</u> as used in paragraph 11?

   F Happy

   G Discouraged

   H Hard-shelled, dry seeds

   J Crazy

---

5   The author's purpose for writing this story is likely —

   A to show that dogs do not like people

   B to show that people are selfish

   C to show that dogs do not always think what we expect

   D to show that dogs really like boys

---

6   The purpose of the illustration is likely —

   F to illustrate the friendship between the boy and his dog

   G to show that Butch loves to play fetch

   H to create an image for the reader

   J to show that dogs like to play in parks

GO ON ➜

Name: _____ Date: _____

It's a Dog's Life *(cont.)*

7   Based on the information in the story, the reader can conclude that —

   A Butch loves everything about his life with Andy.

   B Butch gets frustrated with his family.

   C Butch loves to play fetch every day.

   D Butch got to eat at the family dinner table.

---

8   The author most likely wrote this to —

   F inform

   G explain

   H entertain

   J persuade

Name: _____ Date: _____

Windy Nights

by Robert Louis Stevenson

Directions: Read this poem and respond to the questions on pages 88–90.

Whenever the moon and stars are set,
  Whenever the wind is high,
All night long in the dark and wet,
  A man goes riding by.
5 Late in the night when the fires are out,
Why does he gallop and gallop about?

Whenever the trees are crying aloud,
  And ships are tossed at sea,
By, on the highway, low and loud,
10 By at the gallop goes he.
By at the gallop he goes, and then
By he comes back at the gallop again.

GO ON ➡

Name: _____ Date: _____

Windy Nights (cont.)

Directions: Read each question carefully. Record the correct answer on your answer sheet.

1   Read lines 3–4 from the poem.

> *All night long in the dark and wet,*
> *A man goes riding by.*

What does the man represent?

A A horseback rider

B The rain

C The movement of air

D The trees

2   The author uses figurative language about —

F the moon and stars

G trees

H fires

J ships

3   Which line from the poem is an example of figurative language?

A *Whenever the moon and stars are set*

B *Late in the night when the fires are out*

C *And ships are tossed at sea*

D *Whenever the trees are crying aloud*

GO ON

Name: _____ Date: _____

Windy Nights (cont.)

4 How does the man move on his horse in the poem?

F Very quietly

G Back and forth

H In the daytime

J With a high scream

---

5 Which word in the poem best helps you to visualize the man's movement through the town?

A Gallop

B Loud

C Moon

D Highway

---

6 The whole poem is a metaphor for —

F a foggy night

G a storm

H a horseback rider

J the wind

GO ON

Name: _____ Date: _____

Windy Nights *(cont.)*

7 Which of the following is an adjective used to describe the wind?

    A Gallop

    B High

    C Tossed

    D Highway

---

8 Which lines of the poem rhyme?

    F Lines 2 and 4

    G Lines 3 and 4

    H Lines 1 and 8

    J Lines 6 and 7

Name: _____ Date: _____

A Pleasant Day

by Eliza Lee Cabot Follen

Directions: Read this poem and respond to the questions on pages 92–94.

Come, my children, come away,
For the sun shines bright today;
Little children, come with me,
Birds and brooks and flowers see;
5   Get your hats and come away,
For it is a <u>pleasant</u> day.

Everything is laughing, singing,
All the pretty flowers are springing;
See the kittens, full of fun,
10   Tumbling in the brilliant sun;
Children, too, may skip and play,
For it is a pleasant day.

Bring the hoop and bring the ball,
Come with happy faces all;
15   Let us make a merry ring,
Talk and laugh and dance and sing.
Quickly, quickly, come away,
For it is a pleasant day.

GO ON

Name: _____ Date: _____

A Pleasant Day *(cont.)*

Directions: Read each question carefully. Record the correct answer on your answer sheet.

1   What makes the author believe that it is a pleasant day?

   A *Children, too, may skip and play*

   B *Get your hats and come away*

   C *For the sun shines bright today*

   D *Let us make a merry ring*

---

2   The poem would most likely make the reader feel —

   F Happy

   G Sad

   H Fearful

   J Angry

---

3   Which form of poetry is "A Pleasant Day"?

   A Narrative poetry

   B Humorous poetry

   C Lyrical poetry

   D Free verse

GO ON

Name: _____ Date: _____

A Pleasant Day *(cont.)*

4 Which word is the best synonym for <u>pleasant</u>?

    F Nice

    G Hopeful

    H Perfect

    J Cloudy

---

5 What does the author want the children to notice?

    A *Come with happy faces all*

    B *Talk and laugh and dance and sing*

    C *Birds and brooks and flowers see*

    D *Quickly, quickly, come away*

---

6 Which line from the poem expresses an opinion?

    F *Children, too, may skip and play*

    G *Get your hats and come away*

    H *Bring the hoop and bring the ball*

    J *For it is a pleasant day*

GO ON ➡

Name: _____ Date: _____

A Pleasant Day (cont.)

7 Which word from the poem expresses an emotion?

A Pretty

B Happy

C Brilliant

D Quickly

---

8 Look at the diagram.

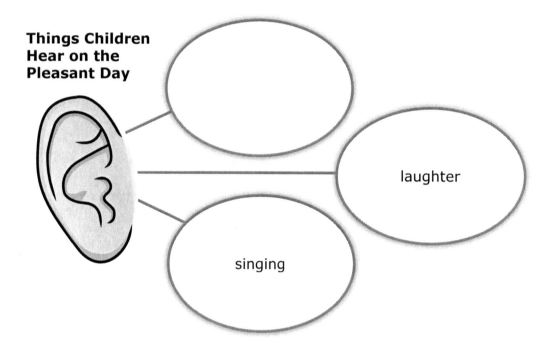

Things Children Hear on the Pleasant Day

laughter

singing

Which of the following completes the diagram?

F Tumbling

G Shouting

H Beauty

J Talking

Name: _____ Date: _____

The Plumpuppets

by Christopher Morley

Directions: Read this poem and respond to the questions on pages 96–98.

When little heads <u>weary</u> have gone to their bed,
When all the good nights and the prayers have been said,
Of all the good fairies that send babes to rest
The little <u>Plumpuppets</u> are those I love best.

5 If your pillow is lumpy, or hot, thin, and flat,
The little Plumpuppets know just what they're at.
They plump up the pillow, all soft, cool, and fat.
The little Plumpuppets <u>plump up it</u>!

The little Plumpuppets are fairies of beds.
10 They have nothing to do but to watch sleepyheads.
They turn down the sheets, and they tuck you in tight.
And then dance on your pillow to wish you good night!

GO ON ➡

Name: _____ Date: _____

The Plumpuppets (cont.)

Directions: Read each question carefully. Record the correct answer on your answer sheet.

1 What is a <u>Plumpuppet</u>?

    A A fairy

    B A puppet

    C A sleeping child

    D A pillow

---

2 The job of a Plumpuppet is to —

    F wave wands that make children fall asleep

    G sing lullabies to children

    H make children comfortable so they fall asleep

    J leave money under children's pillows

---

3 Which line from the poem describes how Plumpuppets do their jobs?

    A *The little Plumpuppets are fairies of beds.*

    B *They plump up the pillow, all soft, cool, and fat.*

    C *And then dance on your pillow to wish you good night!*

    D *When little heads weary have gone to their bed,*

© Shell Education

Name: _____ Date: _____

The Plumpuppets (cont.)

4   Read this dictionary entry for the word <u>weary</u>.

> **weary** \weer-ee\ *adjective*
> **1.** bored
> **2.** annoyed
> **3.** tired
> **4.** impatient

Which meaning of <u>weary</u> is used in the first line of the poem?

F   Meaning 1

G   Meaning 2

H   Meaning 3

J   Meaning 4

---

5   What does the author mean by the phrase <u>plump up it</u>?

A   Making a mattress softer

B   Turning down bed sheets

C   Jumping on a bed

D   Fluffing up a pillow

---

6   Which line of the poem expresses the author's opinion about Plumpuppets?

F   *The little Plumpuppets know just what they're at.*

G   *The little Plumpuppets are those I love best.*

H   *The little Plumpuppets plump up it!*

J   *They have nothing to do but to watch sleepyheads.*

GO ON

Name: _____ Date: _____

The Plumpuppets (cont.)

7 From the poem the reader can conclude that —

    A children are not aware of Plumpuppets

    B children are afraid of Plumpuppets

    C children like Plumpuppets

    D children need more comfortable beds

---

8 What can be concluded about fairies?

    F They like to sleep beside children.

    G They all help children go to sleep.

    H There are different kinds of fairies.

    J All fairies are Plumpuppets.

Name: _____ Date: _____

Mr. Macklin's Jack O'Lantern

by David McCord

Directions: Read this poem and respond to the questions on pages 100–102.

Mr. Macklin takes his knife
And carves the yellow pumpkin face:
Three holes bring eyes and nose to life;
The mouth has thirteen teeth in place.

5 Then Mr. Macklin, just for fun,
Transfers the corn cob pipe from his
Wry mouth to Jack's, and everyone
Dies laughing! O what fun it is!

Till Mr. Macklin <u>draws the shade</u>
10 And lights the candle in Jack's skull
Then all the inside dark is made
As spooky and as horrorful

As Halloween, and creepy crawl
The shadows on the tool-house floor.
15 With Jack's face dancing on the wall.
Oh, Mr. Macklin! Where's the door?

GO ON ➡

Name: _____ Date: _____

Mr. Macklin's Jack O'Lantern *(cont.)*

Directions: Read each question carefully. Record the correct answer on your answer sheet.

1   Which two emotions does the poem communicate?

   A Excitement and joy

   B Anger and fear

   C Joy and fright

   D Happiness and anger

_____

2   What is another term for <u>draws the shade</u> as used in line 9?

   F Pulls down the blind

   G Draws a dark picture

   H Turns off the lights

   J Lights a candle

_____

3   What does everyone do when Mr. Macklin puts a pipe in the pumpkin's mouth?

   A They scream.

   B They run away.

   C They hide.

   D They laugh.

Name: _____ Date: _____

Mr. Macklin's Jack O'Lantern *(cont.)*

4 What action occurs that changes the mood in the poem?

    F The room gets dark and Mr. Macklin lights a candle.

    G Mr. Macklin puts the Jack O'Lantern in the window.

    H Mr. Macklin puts a pipe in Jack's mouth.

    J Mr. Macklin carves the pumpkin.

---

5 The mood in the house changes from —

    A scary to fun

    B happy to sad

    C fun to scary

    D sad to happy

---

6 The purpose of the illustration is likely —

    F to show that people feel afraid

    G to show that Halloween is fun

    H to teach the reader how to carve a pumpkin

    J to show what Jack looks like

GO ON ➡

Name: _____ Date: _____

Mr. Macklin's Jack O'Lantern *(cont.)*

7   What happens after Mr. Macklin carves the face?

   A   He lights a candle.

   B   He adds a corn cob pipe.

   C   He puts it in the window.

   D   Everyone laughs.

---

8   What do the shadows of Jack's face make people want to do?

   F   Die laughing

   G   Hide

   H   Leave

   J   Go trick-or-treating

Name: _____ Date: _____

Answer Sheet

Practice Exercise: _____

Directions: Fill in each correct answer.

1 (A) (B) (C) (D)
2 (F) (G) (H) (J)
3 (A) (B) (C) (D)
4 (F) (G) (H) (J)
5 (A) (B) (C) (D)
6 (F) (G) (H) (J)
7 (A) (B) (C) (D)
8 (F) (G) (H) (J)

- -

Name: _____ Date: _____

Answer Sheet

Practice Exercise: _____

Directions: Fill in each correct answer.

1 (A) (B) (C) (D)
2 (F) (G) (H) (J)
3 (A) (B) (C) (D)
4 (F) (G) (H) (J)
5 (A) (B) (C) (D)
6 (F) (G) (H) (J)
7 (A) (B) (C) (D)
8 (F) (G) (H) (J)

Correlation to Assessed Standards

The following chart correlates each question in this book to its designated eligible TEKS.

Practice Exercise Title	Item Number	Reporting Category	Content Student Expectation	Readiness/Supporting
Bats on the Brink (pages 11–15)	1	3	3.13.A Fig.19.E	Readiness
	2	3	3.13.A Fig.19.E	Readiness
	3	3	3.13.A	Readiness
	4	3	3.13 Fig.19.D	Readiness
	5	1	3.4.B	Readiness
	6	3	3.16	Readiness
	7	3	3.13.D	Readiness
	8	3	3.13.B	Readiness
The Scoop on Sugar (pages 16–21)	1	3	3.13.A Fig.19.D	Readiness
	2	3	3.13.A	Readiness
	3	3	3.13.A	Readiness
	4	3	3.13.A Fig.19.E	Readiness
	5	1	3.4.B	Readiness
	6	3	3.15.B	Supporting
	7	3	3.13.A	Readiness
	8	1	3.4.B	Readiness
A Woman Up a Tree (pages 22–26)	1	3	3.13.A	Readiness
	2	3	3.13.B	Readiness
	3	3	3.13.C	Readiness
	4	3	3.13.B Fig.19.D	Readiness
	5	1	3.4.B	Readiness
	6	3	3.16	Supporting
	7	1	3.4.B	Readiness
	8	3	3.13.A Fig.19.E	Readiness
The Coral Reef Crisis (pages 27–31)	1	3	3.13.C	Readiness
	2	3	3.13.B Fig.19.D	Readiness
	3	3	3.13.A Fig.19.E	Readiness
	4	3	3.13.A	Readiness
	5	3	3.13.B Fig.19.D	Readiness
	6	3	3.16	Supporting
	7	3	3.13.A	Readiness
	8	3	3.13.B Fig.19.E	Readiness
Undersea Volcanoes (pages 32–36)	1	3	3.13.A	Readiness
	2	3	3.13.B	Readiness
	3	3	3.13.B	Readiness
	4	3	3.13.A	Readiness
	5	1	3.4.B	Readiness
	6	3	3.16	Supporting
	7	3	3.13.A	Readiness
	8	3	3.13.A Fig.19.E	Readiness

Correlation to Assessed Standards *(cont.)*

Practice Exercise Title	Item Number	Reporting Category	Content Student Expectation	Readiness/Supporting
She Gives Them Food for Thought (pages 37–40)	1	3	3.13.A	Readiness
	2	3	3.13.A	Readiness
	3	3	3.13.A	Readiness
	4	3	3.13.A Fig.19.D	Readiness
	5	3	3.13.A Fig.19.D	Readiness
	6	3	3.16	Supporting
	7	1	3.4.B	Readiness
	8	3	3.13.A	Readiness
For Sale: Rare and Stolen Pets (pages 41–45)	1	1	3.4.B	Readiness
	2	1	3.4.B	Readiness
	3	3	3.13.A	Readiness
	4	3	3.13.B Fig.19.D	Readiness
	5	3	3.13.C	Readiness
	6	3	3.13.A Fig.19.D	Readiness
	7	3	3.13.A Fig.19.D	Readiness
	8	3	3.13.B	Readiness
Threads of Kindness (pages 46–49)	1	1	3.4.B	Readiness
	2	3	3.13.B	Readiness
	3	3	3.13.A	Readiness
	4	3	3.13.A	Readiness
	5	3	3.13.B Fig.19.D	Readiness
	6	3	3.16	Supporting
	7	3	3.13.B	Readiness
	8	3	3.13.C	Readiness
The Long Trail (pages 50–53)	1	2	3.2.B	Supporting
	2	2	3.8.A Fig.19.D	Readiness
	3	2	3.8.A	Readiness
	4	1	3.4.B	Readiness
	5	2	3.8.A Fig.19.D	Readiness
	6	2	3.16	Supporting
	7	2	3.8.A Fig.19.D	Readiness
	8	2	3.8.A Fig.19.D	Readiness
Paul Bunyan (pages 54–57)	1	2	3.8.B	Readiness
	2	2	3.5.A	Supporting
	3	2	3.8.B	Readiness
	4	1	3.4.B	Readiness
	5	2	3.8.A Fig.19.D	Readiness
	6	2	3.16	Supporting
	7	2	3.8.A Fig.19.D	Readiness
	8	2	3.2.B	Supporting

Correlation to Assessed Standards *(cont.)*

Practice Exercise Title	Item Number	Reporting Category	Content Student Expectation	Readiness/Supporting
Go Fly a Kite! (pages 58–62)	1	1	3.4.B	Readiness
	2	2	3.8.B	Readiness
	3	2	3.8.B	Readiness
	4	2	3.8.A Fig.19.D	Readiness
	5	2	3.8.A Fig.19.D	Readiness
	6	2	3.16	Supporting
	7	2	3.8.B	Readiness
	8	2	3.8.B	Readiness
A Bedouin Tale (pages 63–67)	1	2	3.8.A Fig.19.D	Readiness
	2	2	3.8.B	Readiness
	3	2	3.5.A	Supporting
	4	2	3.8.B	Readiness
	5	2	3.8.B	Readiness
	6	2	3.16	Supporting
	7	2	3.5.A	Supporting
	8	2	3.8.B	Readiness
The Lion and the Wild Boar (pages 68–71)	1	2	3.8.A Fig.19.D	Readiness
	2	2	3.5.A	Supporting
	3	2	3.5.A	Supporting
	4	1	3.4.B	Readiness
	5	2	3.8.A Fig.19.D	Readiness
	6	2	3.8.B	Readiness
	7	2	3.2.B	Supporting
	8	2	3.8.B	Readiness
Racing a Tornado (pages 72–76)	1	2	3.10.A	Supporting
	2	2	3.10.A	Supporting
	3	2	3.16	Supporting
	4	2	3.5.A	Supprting
	5	1	3.4.C	Readiness
	6	2	3.16	Supporting
	7	2	3.16	Supporting
	8	2	3.8.A	Readiness
The Treasure Hunt (pages 77–81)	1	2	3.8.B	Readiness
	2	2	3.8.B	Readiness
	3	2	3.8.B	Readiness
	4	2	3.8.B	Readiness
	5	2	3.5.A	Supporting
	6	2	3.16	Supporting
	7	2	3.8.A Fig.19.D	Readiness
	8	2	3.8.A	Readiness

Correlation to Assessed Standards *(cont.)*

Practice Exercise Title	Item Number	Reporting Category	Content Student Expectation	Readiness/Supporting
It's a Dog's Life (pages 82–86)	1	2	3.8.A Fig.19.D	Readiness
	2	2	3.8.A Fig.19.D	Readiness
	3	2	3.8.A Fig.19.D	Readiness
	4	1	3.4.B	Readiness
	5	2	3.8.A Fig.19.D	Readiness
	6	2	3.16	Supporting
	7	2	3.8.B	Readiness
	8	2	3.8.A Fig.19.D	Readiness
Windy Nights (pages 87–90)	1	2	3.6.A	Supporting
	2	2	3.10.A	Supporting
	3	2	3.10.A	Supporting
	4	2	3.10.A	Supporting
	5	2	3.10.A	Supporting
	6	2	3.10.A	Supporting
	7	2	3.10.A	Supporting
	8	2	3.6.A	Supporting
A Pleasant Day (pages 91–94)	1	2	3.6.A Fig.19.D	Readiness
	2	2	3.6.A	Supporting
	3	2	3.6.A	Supporting
	4	1	3.4.C	Supporting
	5	2	3.6.A Fig.19.D	Readiness
	6	2	3.2.B	Supporting
	7	2	3.2.B	Supporting
	8	2	3.10.A	Supporting
The Plumpuppets (pages 95–98)	1	2	3.2.B	Supporting
	2	2	3.2.B	Supporting
	3	2	3.2.B	Supporting
	4	1	3.4.B	Readiness
	5	1	3.4.B	Readiness
	6	2	3.6.A Fig.19.D	Readiness
	7	2	3.8.B	Readiness
	8	2	3.8.B	Readiness
Mr. Macklin's Jack O'Lantern (pages 99–102)	1	2	3.10.A	Supporting
	2	1	3.4.C	Supporting
	3	2	3.2.B	Supporting
	4	2	3.10.A	Supporting
	5	2	3.10.A	Supporting
	6	2	3.16	Supporting
	7	2	3.2.B	Supporting
	8	2	3.2.B	Supporting

Testing Tips

Reading

READ more nonfiction texts with students!

Writing

Encourage students to **SHOW** what they know with text-based **PROOF**!

How Do I Help Students Prepare for Today's Tests?

Mathematics

Help students **EXPLAIN** what's in their brains and **CONNECT** mathematics to the real world!

Listening

DISCUSS what you read! **ANALYZE** what you think! **SYNTHESIZE** information!!

Testing Tips *(cont.)*

Jail the Detail!		Highlight, underline, or circle the details in the questions. This helps FOCUS on what the question is asking.
Be Slick and Predict!		Predict what the answer is BEFORE you read the choices!
Slash the Trash!		Read ALL the answer choices. "Trash" the choices that you know are incorrect.
Plug It In! Plug It In!		Once you choose an answer, PLUG IT IN! Make sure your answer makes sense, especially with vocabulary and math.
Be Smart with Charts! Zap the Maps!		Charts and maps provide information that you can use to answer some questions. Analyze ALL information before answering a question!
Extra! Extra! Read All About It!		If the directions say read…READ! Pay close attention to signal words in the directions, such as *explain*, *interpret*, and *compare*.
If You Snooze, You Might Lose!		Do not leave questions unanswered. Answering questions increases your chances of getting correct answers!
Check It Out!		After you complete the test, go back and check your work!

References Cited

Conley, David T. 2014. "Common Core Development and Substance." *Social Policy Report* 28 (2): 1–15.

Kornhaber, Mindy L., Kelly Griffith, and Alison Tyler. 2014. "It's Not Education by Zip Code Anymore—But What is It? Conceptions of Equity under the Common Core." *Education Policy Analysis Archives* 22 (4): 1–26. doi:10.14507/epaa.v22n4.2014.

Texas Education Agency. 2014. *State of Texas Assessment of Academic Readiness: A Parent's Guide to the Student Testing Program.* TEA: Texas.

Wiley, Terrence G., and Wayne E. Wright. 2004. "Against the Undertow: Language-Minority Education Policy and Politics in the 'Age of Accountability.'" *Educational Policy*, 18 (1): 142–168. doi:10.1177/0895904803260030.

Answer Key

Bats on the Brink (pages 11–15)

1. C
2. H
3. D
4. J
5. D
6. F
7. B
8. G

The Scoop on Sugar
(pages 16–21)

1. A
2. J
3. C
4. F
5. B
6. J
7. A
8. H

A Woman Up a Tree
(pages 22–26)

1. A
2. G
3. B
4. J
5. A
6. H
7. C
8. G

The Coral Reef Crisis
(pages 27–31)

1. D
2. H
3. A
4. F
5. C
6. F
7. B
8. H

Undersea Volcanoes
(pages 32–36)

1. A
2. G
3. D
4. H
5. B
6. F
7. A
8. G

She Gives Them Food for Thought (pages 37–40)

1. B
2. H
3. D
4. J
5. C
6. H
7. B
8. F

For Sale: Rare and Stolen Pets
(pages 41–45)

1. D
2. H
3. B
4. H
5. A
6. F
7. B
8. J

Threads of Kindness
(pages 46–49)

1. A
2. H
3. B
4. G
5. D
6. F
7. C
8. F

The Long Trail (pages 50–53)

1. D
2. G
3. B
4. H
5. A
6. F
7. D
8. J

Answer Key *(cont.)*

Paul Bunyan (pages 54–57)

1. B
2. J
3. B
4. J
5. C
6. H
7. C
8. G

Go Fly a Kite! (pages 58–62)

1. B
2. J
3. A
4. H
5. C
6. F
7. D
8. F

A Bedouin Tale (pages 63–67)

1. B
2. H
3. D
4. G
5. B
6. J
7. B
8. H

The Lion and the Wild Boar (pages 68–71)

1. A
2. H
3. A
4. G
5. D
6. H
7. B
8. H

Racing a Tornado (pages 72–76)

1. C
2. G
3. A
4. J
5. C
6. G
7. D
8. H

The Treasure Hunt (pages 77–81)

1. B
2. J
3. D
4. H
5. A
6. H
7. C
8. G

It's a Dog's Life (pages 82–86)

1. D
2. J
3. B
4. J
5. C
6. H
7. B
8. H

Windy Nights (pages 87–90)

1. C
2. G
3. D
4. G
5. A
6. J
7. B
8. F

A Pleasant Day (pages 91–94)

1. C
2. F
3. C
4. F
5. C
6. J
7. B
8. J

The Plumpuppets (pages 95–98)

1. A
2. H
3. B
4. H
5. D
6. G
7. A
8. H

Mr. Macklin's Jack O'Lantern (pages 99–102)

1. C
2. F
3. D
4. F
5. C
6. J
7. B
8. H